Watching Dolphins in the Oceans

Elizabeth Miles

Heinemann
LIBRARY

www.heinemann.co.uk/library
Visit our website to find out more information about Heinemann Library books.

To order:

☎ Phone 44 (0) 1865 888066

▤ Send a fax to 44 (0) 1865 314091

💻 Visit the Heinemann Bookshop at www.heinemann.co.uk/library to browse our catalogue and order online.

First published in Great Britain by Heinemann Library, Halley Court, Jordan Hill, Oxford OX2 8EJ, part of Harcourt Education. Heinemann is a registered trademark of Harcourt Education Ltd.

Editorial: Nancy Dickmann and Sarah Chappelow
Design: Ron Kamen and edesign
Illustrations: Martin Sanders
Picture Research: Maria Joannou and Christine Martin
Production: Camilla Crask
Originated by Modern Age
Printed and bound in Italy by Printer Trento srl

ISBN 0 431 19071 2
10 09 08 07 06
10 9 8 7 6 5 4 3 2 1

British Library Cataloguing in Publication Data
Miles, Elizabeth
Watching dolphins in the oceans. – (Wild world)
599.5'317
A full catalogue record for this book is available from the British Library.

Acknowledgements
The Publishers would like to thank the following for permission to reproduce the following photographs: Alamy pp. **7** (Stephen Frink Collection), **29** (Stephen Frink Collection); Ardea pp. **4** (Augusto Stanzani), **21** (Tom and Pat Leeson), **22, 23** (Augusto Stanzani), **28** (Ralf Kiefner); Bruce Coleman p. **19** (Jorg & Petra Wegner); Corbis p. **27** (Guigo Constant); FLPA pp. **12** (Tui de Roy), **20** (Michael Gore); Getty Images pp. **8, 9**; Nature PL pp. **18** (Doug Perrine), **26** (Jeff Rotman); PhotoLibrary.com pp. **5** (IFA-Bilderteam Gmbh), **10** (Gerard Soury), **11** (David Fleetham), **13** (Daniel Cox), **14** (IFA-Bilderteam Gmbh), **15** (Norbert Wu), **16** (Pacific Stock), **24** (Konrad Wothe), **25** (Konrad Wothe); Zefa p .**17** (Masterfile).Cover photographs of dolphins reproduced with permission of Seapics/Ingrid Visser.

The publishers would like to thank Michael Bright of the BBC Natural History Unit for his assistance in the preparation of this book.

Every effort has been made to contact copyright holders of any material reproduced in this book. Any omissions will be rectified in subsequent printings if notice is given to the publishers. The paper used to print this book comes from sustainable resources.

Contents

Meet the dolphins 4

Underwater homes 6

There's a dolphin! 8

Blowholes 10

Swimming in the ocean 12

Ocean food 14

Migration .16

Living together 18

Finding a mate 20

Babies 22

Young calves 24

Dolphins in danger 26

Tracker's guide 28

Glossary 30

Find out more 31

Index 32

Words written in bold, **like this**, are explained in the glossary.

Meet the dolphins

This is the ocean, the home of bottlenose dolphins. Dolphins live in oceans, rivers, and lakes around the world. They are not fish. They are **mammals**, like us.

▶▶ *Dolphins spend most of their time swimming under water.*

There are 32 kinds of dolphin that live in the ocean. We are going to watch bottlenose dolphins. You often see these in marine parks, but most live in the wild.

Although they are called whales, killer whales are part of the dolphin family.

Underwater homes

Bottlenose dolphins live in oceans in many parts of the world. Many of them live off the east **coast** of North America. The water is not too cold there.

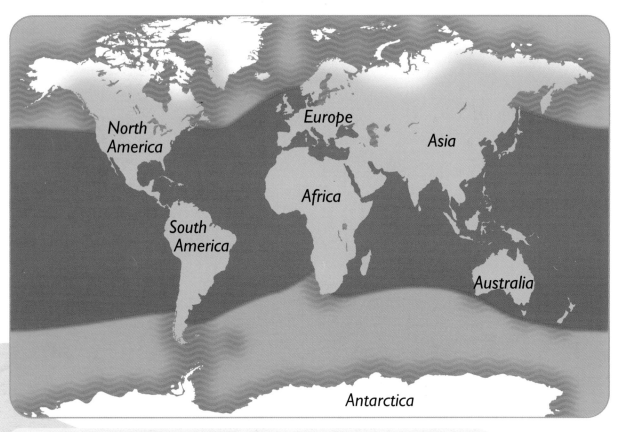

Key ● This colour shows where dolphins live in the oceans.

▲ *Bottlenose dolphins are friendly and do not
mind if people are close by.*

Many bottlenose dolphins stay close to the
coast. They can catch plenty of fish here,
without diving too deep. They often swim
in bays or **harbours**.

7

There's a dolphin!

Spotting a bottlenose is very exciting. Its skin looks smooth and rubbery. Under the skin, there is a layer of fat called blubber. It keeps the dolphin warm.

▶▶ *The bottlenose got its name because people think its nose, or snout, is shaped like a bottle.*

▼ A bottlenose's smooth-shaped body helps it glide through the water.

Bottlenoses are dark grey. They have a light grey patch on their belly. Their colour matches the dark ocean water. This helps them to hide from **predators**.

Blowholes

Dolphins cannot breathe under water like fish can. Dolphins have **lungs**, like people do. They have to come up for air.

▼ *Dolphins come up to breathe every two to four minutes.*

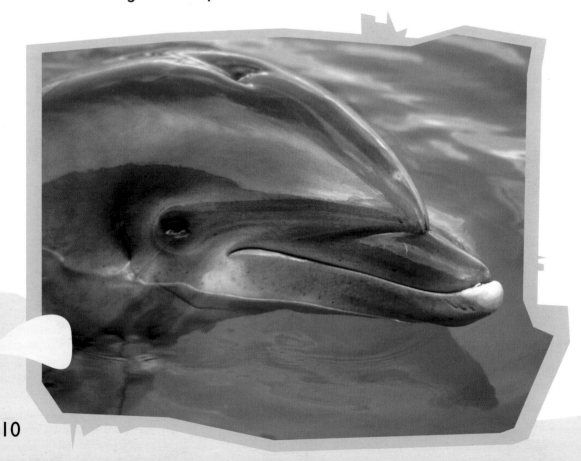

A dolphin breathes through a blowhole on the top of its head. It closes the blowhole when it dives under water. Water cannot get in when the blowhole is closed.

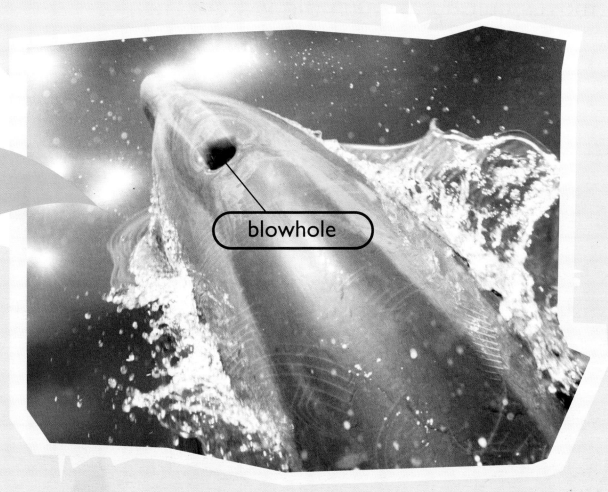

blowhole

▲ *A dolphin's blowhole is like a **nostril**.*

Swimming in the ocean

Dolphins swim by flapping their tail and **flukes** up and down. Their smooth body moves quickly through the water. They use their **flippers** to turn and to stop.

▼ *The **fin** on the bottlenose's back stops the dolphin from rolling around in the water.*

flipper

fin

flukes

Bottlenoses are very good at jumping. Sometimes they jump for fun. When they land, the splash lets other dolphins know where they are.

▲ *Bottlenoses can take a breath of air when they jump.*

Ocean food

Bottlenoses eat fish and squid. They grab their **prey** with their teeth. They do not chew their food. Instead, they swallow it whole.

▼ *Dolphins learn to eat fish that is good for them, such as mullet.*

To find fish to eat, dolphins make clicking noises. The sound of the clicks bounces off the fish as an **echo**. This tells dolphins where the fish are.

▲ *The echo tells the dolphins if there is anything there, like a **shoal** of fish to eat.*

Migration

In summer the bottlenoses swim north. There are more fish to eat there. The dolphins swim for days to reach new places to feed.

▼ *People sometimes follow dolphins on their journey in boats.*

⬆ When bottlenose dolphins migrate, they travel in large groups, called herds, of up to 100.

In winter, there are fewer fish to eat. The bottlenoses swim south again. They **migrate** north and south every year.

Living together

Dolphins usually live in small groups called pods. There are about seven dolphins in a pod. If one dolphin is ill, the others will help it stay afloat.

▼ *A pod of dolphins hunts together. These dolphins are rounding up a **shoal** of fish to eat.*

▲ *Groups of dolphins like to swim and jump together.*

Dolphins make whistling and clicking noises to **communicate** with each other. They also send messages by slapping their **flukes** on the surface of the water.

Finding a mate

In autumn it is time for **male** dolphins to find **females** to **mate** with. They may have to fight for a female. Female dolphins are called cows.

▼ *Male dolphins are called bulls. These bulls are fighting over a female.*

The male that wins the fight goes to the female. Before mating, the male and female might swim together. They may touch **flippers** or even **butt** heads.

▼ *It is hard to see which is the bull and which is the cow.*

Babies

In autumn, one year after she has **mated**, the **female** bottlenose gives birth. A baby dolphin is called a calf. Calves are paler than adults.

▼ *Calves are born tail first and then swim to the surface to take their first breath of air.*

▲ *Mother dolphins stay close to their calves.*

The mother can produce milk. She feeds
milk to her calf for more than a year. She
will look after the calf for many years.

Young calves

The calf soon learns to swim about. It learns to recognize the sound of its mother's whistle. When the mother whistles, the calf will come to her side.

A young calf often swims beside its mother. **Predators** *cannot easily see it there.*

Groups of **females** often live together. They help look after each other's calves. One mother goes off to hunt, while the others babysit her calf.

⏫ *In a few years these calves will be old enough to leave their mothers.*

25

Dolphins in danger

Calves learn to protect themselves from sharks and **orcas**. Dolphins use their head as a battering ram to fight off these **predators**.

Sharks sometimes wait for dolphins to swim by.

▶▶ *A diver will help this dolphin get free. Many others die in nets like these.*

Some people kill dolphins for food. Lots of dolphins get stuck in fishing nets. If a calf survives these dangers, it should live to be about 30 years old.

Tracker's guide

When you want to watch animals in the wild, you need to find them first. Dolphins can be hard to find because they live in the oceans.

⏫ *You must look carefully to spot a dolphin. They often swim at the front of big boats.*

⬆ Some people go on dolphin-watching trips. Bottlenose dolphins are well known for being friendly to people.

Glossary

butt hit something with your head

coast edge of the land, where it meets the sea

communicate pass on information. Talking is a way of communicating.

echo sound that bounces back so you hear it again

female animal that can become a mother when it is grown up. Girls and women are female people.

fin part that sticks out from the top of a fish, dolphin, or whale

flipper fin that sticks out from the side of a dolphin like an arm

flukes two parts that make up a dolphin's tail

harbour sheltered part of the coast, where boats are often kept

lungs parts inside the body that you use to breathe air in and out

male animal that can become a father when it is grown up. Boys and men are male people.

mammal group of animals that feed their babies their own milk and have some hair on their bodies

mate when male and female animals produce young

migrate travel a long distance, following the same journey every year

nostril hole that you breathe through. Your nose has two nostrils.

orca another name for a killer whale

predator animal that catches and eats other animals for food

prey animal that gets caught and eaten by other animals

shoal group of fish

Find out more

Books

Diving with Dolphins, Nick Arnold (Scholastic, 2004)

Ocean Explorer, Greg Pyers (Raintree, 2004)

Ocean food chains, Emma Lynch (Heinemann Library, 2004)

Sea creatures: Dolphins, Elizabeth Laskey (Heinemann Library, 2003)

Why do animals have wings, fins and flippers? Elizabeth Miles
     (Heinemann Library, 2002)

Whales, Dolphins, and Porpoises, Mark Carwardine
     (Dorling Kindersley, 2002)

Websites

Find out more amazing facts about dolphins at:
http://www.nationalgeographic.com/ngkids/0506/index.html

Disclaimer

All the internet addresses (URLs) given in this book were valid at the time of going to press. However, due to the dynamic nature of the internet, some addresses may have changed, or sites may have ceased to exist since publication. While the author and publishers regret any inconvenience this may cause readers, no responsibility for such changes can be accepted by either the author(s) or the publishers.

Index

autumn 20, 22

blowholes 11
blubber 8

calves 22, 23, 24, 25, 26, 27

echoes 15

flippers 12, 21
flukes 12, 19

harbours 7

jumping 13, 19

killer whales (orcas) 5, 26

lungs 10

mammals 4
mating 20, 21
migration 16, 17

North America 6

pods 18
predators 9, 24, 26

sharks 26
summer 16

winter 17

Titles in the *Wild World* series include:

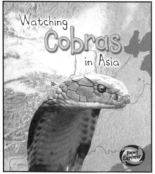

Hardback   0 431 19066 6

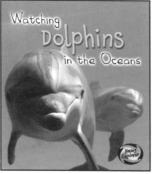

Hardback   0 431 19071 2

Hardback   0 431 19084 4

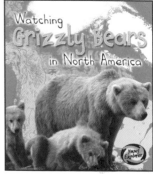

Hardback   0 431 19069 0

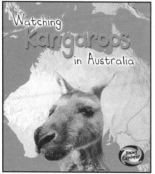

Hardback   0 431 19067 4

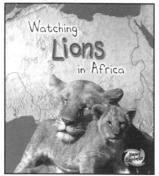

Hardback   0 431 19064 X

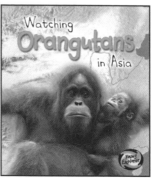

Hardback   0 431 19085 2

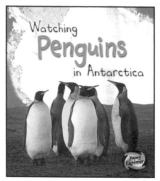

Hardback   0 431 19065 8

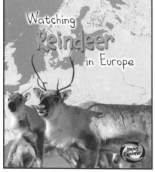

Hardback   0 431 19068 2

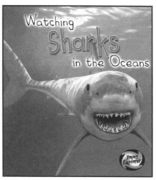

Hardback   0 431 19086 0

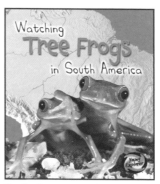

Hardback   0 431 19070 4

Find out about other Heinemann Library titles on our website www.heinemann.co.uk/library